The Lokta Illustrated Bible

Creation

Phil Rawlings

The Lokta Illustrated Bible - Book One - Creation

First published by Phil Rawlings, March 2021.

Art+Design © MMXXI Phil Rawlings. All rights reserved.

First edition 2021.

Hardcover ISBN: 978-9937-0-8057-6
Softcover ISBN: 978-9937-0-8058-3
eBook ISBN: 978-9937-0-8059-0

www.philrawlings.com/books
www.fb.com/PhoolishDesigns
author@philrawlings.com

Authors note:
Some of the verses in this publication are incomplete or paraphrased, for artistic impression.
This book is not a substitute for the genuine **WORD** of **God**. Each illustration has
the corresponding chapter and verse that it represents in the bottom corner.
For full translations visit www.biblegateway.com

*All glory to **HIM**.*

In loving memory of **mum**,
my harshest critic and my biggest supporter,
much loved and missed, never forgotten.

In the beginning...

Before the **world** began, the **WORD** was there.

The **WORD** was with **God**, and the **WORD was God**. He was there with **God** in the beginning. Everything was made **through him**, and **nothing** was made **without him**. In him was **life**.

John 1:1-4

In the **beginning**, **God created** the sky and the earth.

The earth was **empty**. Darkness covered the ocean, and **God's Spirit** moved over the water.

Genesis 1:1-2

Then God said,
"Let there be light!"
And light began to
shine, and it was **good**.

So he separated the **light** from the **darkness**.
God named the light **"day,"** and the darkness **"night"**.

This was the **first day**.

Genesis 1:3-5

Then God said, **"Let there be something to divide the water in two!"** So God made the **air** to divide the water in two, and he named the air **"sky."**

This was the **second day**.

Genesis 1:6-8

Then God said, **"Let the water under the sky be gathered together so the dry land will appear."**

God named the dry land **"earth,"** and he named the water that was gathered together **"seas."**

Genesis 1:9-10

And God said, **"Let the earth grow grass, plants that make grain, and fruit trees. Each plant will make its own kind of seed and grow all over the earth."**

This was the **third day**.

Genesis 1:11-13

Then God said, **"Let there be lights in the sky to separate day from night. They will be used for signs, seasons, days and years."**

So God made a brighter light to **rule the day**

and a smaller light to **rule the night.**

He also made the **stars**. God put all these in the sky to **shine on the earth**. He put them there to **separate** the **light** from the **darkness**.

This was the **fourth day**.

Genesis 1:14-19

Then God said, **"Let the water be filled with living things. And let birds fly in the air above the earth."**

God blessed them and said, **"Have many babies and fill the seas and the skies."**

This was the **fifth day**.

Genesis 1:20-23

Then God said, "Let the earth be filled with animals. And let each produce more of its own kind."

So God made the **wild animals**, the **tame animals** and the small **crawling animals**.

Genesis 1:24-25

Then God said, **"Let us make human beings in our image and likeness. They will be responsible for the fish in the sea, the birds in the sky, and the animals on the earth."**

So God created **male** and **female** in his image, and he blessed them and said, **"Have many children and grow in numbers."**

Genesis 1:26-28

God looked at **everything he had made**, and saw that **it was very good**.

This was the **sixth day**.

Genesis 1:31

ABOUT NEPALESE LOKTA PAPER

Nepalese handmade lokta paper is made from the fibrous inner bark of high elevation Lokta bushes which proliferate in open clusters or colonies on the southern slopes of Nepal's Himalayan forests between 1,600 and 4,000 metres.

Lokta is a non-wood forest product (NWFP) harvested from protected areas (national parks, reserves and conservation areas) and is an important reservoir of biological resources maintained under in situ condition in the unique and diverse Himalayan ecosystems. When harvested, the lokta bush naturally regenerates to a fully grown 4–5 metre plant within 5–7 years, ensuring the paper is truly environmentally friendly.

Historically, the handcrafting of lokta paper occurred in the rural areas of Nepal. Today, raw lokta paper is produced in more than 22 districts in Nepal, but finished lokta paper products are produced only in the Kathmandu Valley and Janakpur.

Lokta paper's durability and resistance to tearing, humidity, insects and mildew have traditionally made it the preferred choice for the recording of official government records and sacred religious texts.

The earliest surviving lokta paper document appears in Nepal's National Archives in Kathmandu in the form of the sacred Buddhist text, the *Karanya Buha Sutra*. Estimated to be between 1,000 and 1,900 years old, The *Karanya Buha Sutra* was written in Lichchhavi script and block printed on lokta paper.

Once the lokta paper is produced it can last for some millenniums (estimated at 2,000–3,500 years).

OTHER BOOKS BY PHIL RAWLINGS

www.philrawlings.com/books

The Twelve Days of Christmas is a book of 12 illustrations depicting the popular carol of the same name. Each spread of the book has a beautiful image made from a collage of Nepalese Lokta Paper, each showing the gifts that the singer received from their 'true love' over the 12 days.

Giving someone all the gifts in the carol today would be pretty expensive! The PNC financial services group's annual Christmas Price Index calculates the cost of all the gifts in the song based on current market rates; 2018's total came to a hefty $39,094.93, or $170,609.46 if you count each mention of an item separately (which would amount to 364 gifts in all).

The first day of Christmas is traditionally Christmas day (the 25th December), and the twelve days ends on 6th January.

Available in paperback and eBook.

A {Phool} in Nepal is a pictoral account of Phil Rawlings' first three months in Nepal.

"I first met Phil (Phool) in 2001. He was working in graphic design and clearly had a promising future. Yet there was within him restlessness that a good job, a nice car, a great collection of DVD's, the latest phone or gadget never truly satisfied. A Christian man sensing that there was "more to life than this". Then God spoke. Phil responded with courage and patience. God had a plan and a purpose for Phil to be in Nepal. Through his step of faith and sacrifice he received much more than he ever dreamed of: a ministry, a sense of purpose, and a wife! How cool is that???

This book reflects Phil's talent in photography yes, but more than that. Anyone can take a photo; tell a story, but knowing what to take, when, and whose story to tell? Now that's a talent. This beautiful book takes you right to the heart of Nepali culture, its deep beauty, history, joys, and sadness too.

Allow the words and pictures to take you there but more than that, to enable you imagine what God might do in your life if you ask, take courage, and a step of faith.

Pray for him. Support him."   *Rev Jon Stannard*

ISBN 978-9937-0-8057-6

CPSIA information can be obtained
at www.ICGtesting.com
Printed in the USA
BVHW091615280321
603524BV00012B/189